JEFFREY DEAN

MW01042744

between the lines
One-Liner Wisdom for Today's

guys

Multnomah Publishers® *Sisters, Oregon*

ONE-LINER WISDOM FOR TODAY'S GUYS
published by Multnomah Publishers *A division of Random House Inc.*
© 2006 by Jeffrey Dean
International Standard Book Number: 1-59052-971-5

Unless otherwise indicated, Scripture quotations are from:
The Holy Bible, New International Version © 1973, 1984 by International Bible Society,
used by permission of Zondervan Publishing House

Other Scripture quotations are from:
The Message © 1993, 1994, 1995, 1996, 2000, 2001, 2002
Used by permission of NavPress Publishing Group

Multnomah is a trademark of Multnomah Publishers,
and is registered in the U.S. Patent and Trademark Office.
The colophon is a trademark of Multnomah Publishers
Printed in Mexico

For information:
MULTNOMAH PUBLISHERS
12265 ORACLE BOULEVARD, SUITE 200
COLORADO SPRINGS, CO 80921

Library of Congress Cataloging-in-Publication Data
Dean, Jeffrey.
  One-liner wisdom for today's guys / Jeffrey Dean.
      p. cm.
  ISBN 1-59052-971-5
  1. Teenage boys--Conduct of life. 2. Teenage boys--Religious life. I. Title.
BJ1671.D43 2006
248.8'32--dc22

                              2006023854

06 07 08 09 10—10 9 8 7 6 5 4 3 2 1 0

# Table of Contents

Introduction

INTRO »

Your teen years are a fast-moving world of instant messages, football games, the opposite sex, pop quizzes, proms, and parents. Some days things get boring, some days intense. But every day, one thing is sure: Your choices matter. In fact, one wrong move can do a lot of damage. That's why you need to keep your future in mind, and ask for help along the way.

One-Liner Wisdom for Today's Guys brings you a fun, easy-to-read resource packed with biblical and practical ideas. In less than a minute a day, you'll find the perspective you need to think clearly, and to live life at its very best.

Of course, this little book won't make all your trials and challenges disappear. But it will help you to think about what really matters in life and invite God to speak His truth and love into your heart. And no life is moving too fast for that!

Chapter 1

MY WALK

Girls. Music. Sports. Your car. Your clothes. What are you living for? What drives you? What motivates you as a man? Every day you choose to either walk the road God has paved for you or the slippery one Satan hopes to entice you to travel. One will lead you to prosperity. The other will lead you nowhere. One will lead you to become the man you were born to be. The other will leave you empty and wanting to be someone other than who you've become. Your life. Your choice. Your walk. **Which direction are you going?**

Right now you are becoming the **man** you will one day be.

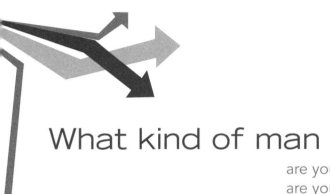

What kind of man

are you becoming?
are you becoming?
are you becoming?
do you want to be?
do you want to be?
do you want to be?

Blessed is the man who does not walk in the counsel of the wicked or stand in the way of sinners or sit in the seat of mockers.

Psalm 1:1

Write a brief description of the man you believe you are today.

Not following God like I desire, follows the crowd, secrets from parents, dirty music and movies, Clean on outside.

Now, write a description of the man you would like to become.

Follow God, stand up for what I believe, act more Christlike (language, actions, etc.)

Are these two different? If so, what can you do to change that?

I need to start doing my daily devotion every day!

What are you living for?

Make a list of all the things in your life that you are passionate about. Most likely, these "things" are what you are living for, whether you realize it or not.

- Music
- Movies
- Popularity/Friends
- Phone/iPod
- God?

Your passions drive your choices.
Your choices shape your lifestyle.
Your lifestyle defines what you live for.

Think about the journey you are on in life. Has it ever occurred to you that you were created for more than you are experiencing right now?

Consider this: Could it be that you are missing out on something bigger, greater, more awesome, challenging, inspiring, and fulfilling than the present?

"I came so they can have real and eternal life, more and better life than they ever dreamed of."

John 10:10 *(The Message)*

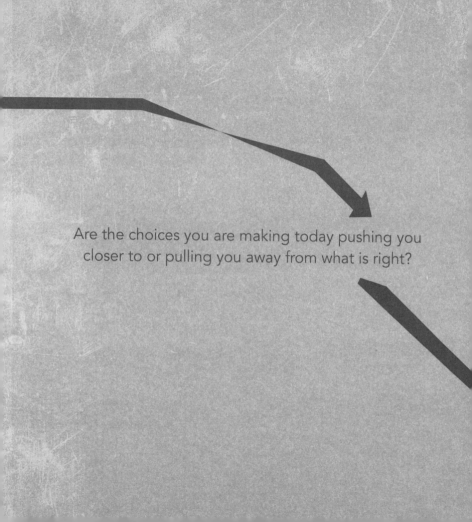

Are the choices you are making today pushing you closer to or pulling you away from what is right?

Sometimes, in order to have what is best, you must be willing to **say no** to what seems good.

It isn't about perfection.

It isn't about success.

It isn't about running.

It isn't about making a name for yourself today.

It isn't about having all the answers.

It isn't about giving up your life.

Do you think Noah knew how to swim?

It is about service.

It is about purpose.

It is about trusting Him with all your questions.

It is about daily walking in His steps.

It is about getting the very best life He has for you.

It's about making the most of today.

When was the last time
you really talked with your parents?

Before picking a girl up
for a date, wash your car.

No matter how innocent it may seem, make no mistake—porn will take you down a dead-end road.

Do not be deceived: God cannot be mocked. A man reaps what he sows. The one who sows to please his sinful nature, from that nature will reap destruction.

Galatians 6:7-8

God doesnt' use perfect people.
He uses people to fulfill his

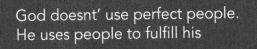

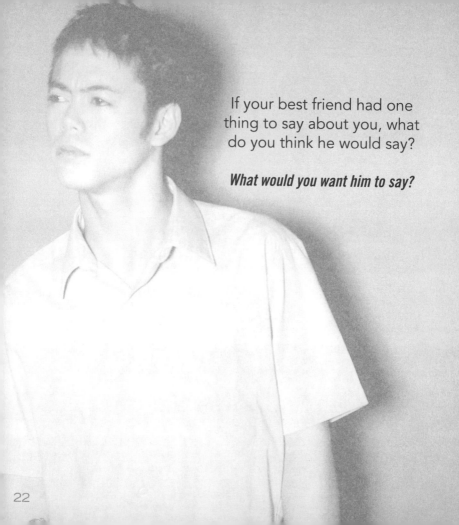

If your best friend had one thing to say about you, what do you think he would say?

What would you want him to say?

22

Make a list of the top five characteristics you want to have.

1. Clean Mind
2. Polite (Teachers)
3. Godly
4. Treat ALL of my friends equally even those not as cool.
5. Stand out from the crowd later on with drugs and alchohol!

Now make a list of five characteristics you presently possess.

1. Dirty (Jokes, language, etc.)
2. Rude
   Unrighteous
4. Blows off "losers"
5. Follows "cool" friends / leads others to do wrong

Do these two lists match? No

If not, what changes do you need to make in your life to allow these two lists to mirror one another?

Delete music app, change the way I think of unpopular people, stand up for God

Chapter 2
MY VALUE

I remember in junior high I was so skinny that when I turned to the side you could hardly see me. I had so many pimples you could literally play connect-the-dots on my face. I wasn't crazy about my appearance then, but I now realize that the Bible says each of us is created in the image of God. He created us exactly as He wants us to be. It's good to know that even when you may not feel very valuable, **God considers you to be of the highest value.** He deemed you valuable enough to pay the highest price possible for your life…pimples and all!

You are valuable enough to die for.

 You were bought at a price.

1 Corinthians 6:20

When confessing sin to God, remember, He loves you and desires to restore you to fellowship with Him. Once you confess, let go of it and walk away.

 Seek God while he's here to be found, pray to him while he's close at hand. Let the wicked abandon their way of life and the evil their way of thinking. Let them come back to God, who is merciful, come back to our God, who is lavish with forgiveness.

Isaiah 55:6–7 *(The Message)*

God loves you so much that He
won't sit idly and allow you to
wallow in the mess of your life.

He daily wants to renew you.

He daily wants to bring you into
closer fellowship with Him.

He daily pursues you.

Will you let Him have you?

Have you talked to God about your life?

It is impossible to know His will for your life
if you do not ask Him.

Don't beat yourself up. The past is the past. If it's forgiven, it's forgotten.

 As far as sunrise is from sunset, he has separated us from our sins.

Psalm 103:12 *(The Message)*

Nothing you do will ever
make God love you any less
than He does right now.

Nothing you do will ever make God love you
any more than He does right now.

Suicide isn't the answer.

Suicide is the absolute worst choice
you can make—that you can never undo.

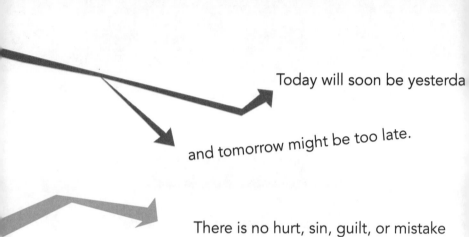

Today will soon be yesterda

and tomorrow might be too late.

There is no hurt, sin, guilt, or mistake
that God can't heal.

Have you ever been caught in a lie? Learn from past mistakes. Don't keep repeating them.

 Do not lie.

Leviticus 19:11

Imagine…

There is an actual army that fights for you. Angels fight for you every day.

The angel of the LORD encamps around those who fear him, and he delivers them.

Psalm 34:7

Satan works extremely hard trying to convince us that we will never be good enough, smart enough, skinny enough, strong enough, manly enough, sexy enough, rich enough, or popular enough.

Am I now trying to win the approval of men, or of God? Or am I trying to please men? If I were still trying to please men, I would not be a servant of Christ.

Galatians 1:10

Chapter 3

MY GOD

You probably know a lot about your best friend, don't you? His likes, dislikes, what makes him tick, and what ticks him off. Why is it that you know so much about this person? You know all about him because you have made it a priority to spend time with him. The same is true when it comes to your relationship with God. How much time do you spend with God each day? **You can never truly know Him without spending time with Him.** Making God a priority in your life takes time, discipline, and commitment. Doing so will be one of the greatest choices you will ever make.

Dear (insert you name here) ,

I know what I'm doing. I have it all planned out—plans to take care of you, not abandon you, plans to give you the future you hope for.

—GOD

If you could e-mail God right now

and ask Him one question,

what would it be?

You can have all the right things by the standards of this world.

1. The right look
2. The right grades
✔ 3. The right GPA
4. The right degree
5. The right job
6. The right girlfriend
✔ 7. The right amount of money
8. The right house on the right side of town
9. The right car
✔ 10. The right everything

But if you have the wrong relationship with your Creator, then
nothing else matters.

The FRUIT of the spirit: love, joy, peace, patience, kindness, goodness, faithfulness, gentleness, and self-control.

From Galatians 5:22–23

Fruit, *not fruits*. Singular, not plural.

This means the 🍒 isn't for picking and choosing.

It isn't about choosing some of the 🍌 and leaving the rest behind.

It's about applying all of the 🍎 to your life.

Never settle for how others interpret the Bible.

Challenge yourself.

Ask questions.

Dig deeper in Scripture.

Find the answers for yourself.

Know what you believe and why you believe it.

See to it that no one takes you captive through hollow and deceptive philosophy, which depends on human tradition and the basic principles of this world rather than on Christ.

Colossians 2:8

God doesn't mind questions. If you've got them, ask them.

 This is the confidence we have in approaching God: that if we ask anything according to his will, he hears us.

1 John 5:14–15

There will be times in life when circumstances overtake you and you have no satisfying answer for why you have to have such a hard time.

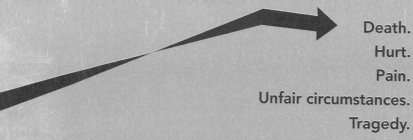

Death.
Hurt.
Pain.
Unfair circumstances.
Tragedy.

During such times, when answers can't be found, remember: God has not left you. God is still in control. God is still God.

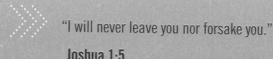

"I will never leave you nor forsake you."

Joshua 1:5

Think of a time when a friend has hurt you.
How did this make you feel?

Lonely, abandoned, rejected, mistreated, spit on,
abused, mocked?

Our sins hurt God.

One of the biggest reasons the world doesn't know Christ is that Christians choose to live inconsistent lives.

Do not cause anyone to stumble.

1 Corinthians 10:32

The world changes, seasons of life change, cultures change, and convictions change.

But this one thing will always remain: God is the ONE absolute truth. He always has been, always will be.

 I the LORD do not change.

Malachi 3:6

Chapter 4

MY STORY

Your first date. Your first drive. Your favorite movie. Your greatest achievement. The winning shot that everyone is still talking about. The girl that makes your heart melt every time you look at her. Defining moments in your life. But what about the moment you gave your heart to Jesus? Do you still remember that moment—where you were when you realized you needed Him? How you felt after He changed your life? There are many moments in the story of your life. But the greatest moment of the story is the moment you stepped from death to life, from sinner to forgiven, from condemned to transformed. This moment not only changed you, but it can be a story used to change others if you will let it. **What is your story?**

Own your story.

You will not be prepared to share the life-changing message about God's love, forgiveness, and salvation through Jesus, His Son, if you do not first own your story.

Know it.

Own it.

Be ready to share it with others.

Someone you know could burn in Hell.

What will you do about that?

There are many who have been killed
for believing in Jesus Christ. Can you imagine dying
for something you believe in?

Would you die for Jesus Christ?

God has created this moment in time exactly for you. This is your moment. **How will you use it?**

You are only one choice away from blowing your witness.

life witness

Definition: the evidence of God in your life
as seen by others watching how you live.

So, how is YOUR life witness?

The life you live **speaks louder**
than the words you say.

Write down the name of someone you know who is not a Christian.

Abraaz

Do you pray for them every day?

_No_

If not, why?

I forget to...

A friend, coach, teacher, principal, boss, mom, brother, cousin, cute chick in algebra class, girlfriend, dad, sister, quarterback on your team, homecoming queen...

EVERYONE you know has one thing in common:

Everyone you know will either go to Heaven or Hell.

There is nothing more certain than death. There is nothing more uncertain than the time of death.

Until you get serious about loving Him, you

will never be serious about living for Him.

How do you talk to a nonbeliever about Jesus?

Start with your story:

1. Who God is to you.

My Savior, Protector, Father

2. What you believe about God.

He sent his Son to die on a cross for ME.

3. What God did for you.

4. What God did to you.

Changed my life/heart

5. How God changed you.

God, Give me the courage to talk with others about you. **The people in my world need you.** Help me to share my Story with them. I want to share my Story with:

1. Abraaz Khan

2. Jake Von Ogden ✓

3. Allie Schank

4. McKenzie Waller

5.

Chapter 5

MY FRIENDS

Friends. We all have them. We all want them. And to a certain extent, we all need them. Of all the things that are important to you in life, your friendships are probably at the top of your list. Do you realize that your friends are more than just people with whom you spend time? Your friends play a powerful role in your life. Why? Because you are greatly influenced by those you spend a lot of time with. How are your friends influencing you? **How are you influencing them?**

Your clothes.

The music on your iPod.

Your favorite sport.

The places you hang.

Your interests.

The movies you watch.

Most likely these favorites are similar to those of your close friends.

Your favorite
TV show.

Do your friends push you closer to
Do your friends push you closer to
Do your friends push you closer to
Do your friends push you closer to
Do your friends push you closer to
Do your friends push you closer to

 or

pull you away from God?
pull you away from God?
pull you away from God?
pull you away from God?
pull you away from God?
pull you away from God?

Think about the one thing that you regret doing more than anything else in your life.

Most likely you did this one thing while in the presence of a friend. At a party. At a friend's house. On a date.

Your friends greatly influence your choices.

As a man, you need godly friendships in your life that will:

✔ encourage you in your relationship with God.

✔ challenge you to go deeper in your walk with God.

✔ understand your dilemmas and temptations as a man.

✔ shoot straight about areas of your life that are not God-honoring.

✔ hold you accountable to live a life that honors God.

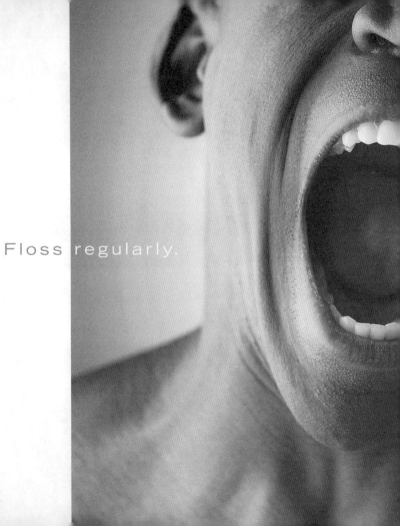

Floss regularly.

He who walks with the wise grows wise, but a companion of fools suffers harm.

Proverbs 13:20

You hang with people who are wise,

the promise:

you will grow wise too!

the warning:

You hang with people who are fools,

you will suffer harm.

God's promise is clear:

A companion of fools
will suffer harm.

Foolish Friend Test #1:

If your friend is not interested in
the Bible, he is a fool.

A fool finds no pleasure
in understanding, but
delights in airing his
own opinions.
                    —Proverbs 18:2

If your best friend
breaks up with a hot girl,
how long
should you wait before
asking her out?

A true friend will never:

✗ ask you to do something contrary to the Bible.

✗ expect you to give in to their every wish.

✗ place you in a compromising situation.

✗ take you to an unsafe environment.

Foolish Friend Test #2:

Your friend is not interested
in pursuing God's ways or
plans for their own life.

Who is wise?
He will realize...the ways
of the Lord are right.
                    —Hosea 14:9

Choosing to place God at the center of your life sometimes means that there may be a relationship you need to walk away from.

Remember: Walking away from a relationship does not mean that you walk away from the person.

If you don't share Jesus with your friends, who will?

Reasons Why We Choose Not To Talk To Our Friends About Jesus

1. Too Embarrassed
2. Afraid of what they might say
3. Afraid of what they might do
4. Don't think it is important enough
5. Don't care

No matter what others say or do,

nothing is ever okay

that is out of the will of God.

A wise friend will be more able to offer you good advice in time of need because they have chosen to follow God's ways, knowing His ways are right.

At the end of your high school career, it really will not matter who you dated, how many baskets you scored in a game, or who signed your yearbook.

What will ultimately matter:

How did you use this moment in time to be a life-changer?

Do your unsaved friends see that the life you live with Jesus is different from the life they live without Him?

Chapter 6

MY LOVE

I still remember the first time I met the girl I would one day marry. I was a freshman in college. She was seated three rows in front of me. I waited until after class, walked up to her, introduced myself, and asked her out on a date. Her one-word reply changed my life forever: "No." I knew she was the one…I just had to convince her. Four long years later, she said yes. And the rest is history. Falling in love with a girl can lead you to do some really crazy things (like asking the same girl out for four years until she finally says yes). But if you are not careful, your heart can also lead you to make choices that seem right in the moment, but eventually lead to great regret. That's why when it comes to love, dating, and sex, God's way is the only way that works. God's way is the only way of **no regrets.**

Until you learn to truly
love God, every other love relationship in
your life will fall short.

Before proposing to a girl—REHEARSE!

Love
never requires an act that is contrary to God's word.

Love
always places another's best interest first.

Love
never forces.

Love
always sticks around.

She may be beautiful. She may be cooler than cool. She may even want to tattoo your name on her body. But be wise. Spend time in prayer, spend time in slow-mo, and spend time making sure you know she's the one.

Sex will never guarantee
that a relationship
will last.

Ten years from now it probably will not matter
what girl you go to prom with.

Ten years from now the choices you make with her on prom night could matter—**a lot.**

Being a man is all about self-control.

Not self-gratification.

No matter how cool, sexy, glamorous, accepted, justifiable, or right the world makes it look, nothing is ever okay that is out of the will of God.

Watch out for people who try to dazzle you with big words and intellectual double-talk. They want to drag you off into endless arguments that never amount to anything. They spread their ideas through the empty traditions of human beings and the empty superstitions of spirit beings. But that's not the way of Christ. Everything of God gets expressed in him, so you can see and hear him clearly. You don't need a telescope, a microscope, or a horoscope to realize the fullness of Christ, and the emptiness of the universe without him. When you come to him, that fullness comes together for you, too. His power extends over everything.

Colossians 2:8–10 *(The Message)*

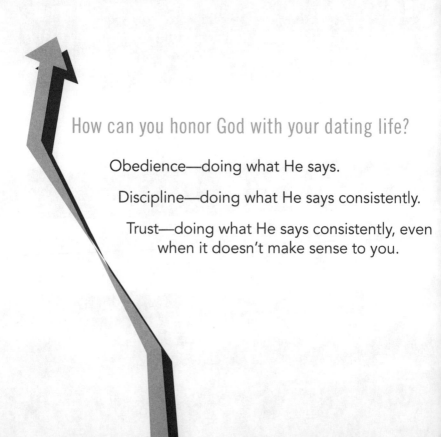

How can you honor God with your dating life?

Obedience—doing what He says.

Discipline—doing what He says consistently.

Trust—doing what He says consistently, even
when it doesn't make sense to you.

Never honk your horn at a girl.

When it comes to your dating choices,

stop and ask:

Will this decision I am about to make **honor** or **dishonor** God?

Will this decision I am about to make **push** this girl closer to or **pull** this girl away from God?

Just because a girl is willing, it doesn't
make the thing she is willing to do right.

Any man can make excuses.
Stop making excuses and start making a difference.

Any relationship that is more important to you
than God will never satisfy you.

Hooking up.

Sex.

Friends with benefits.

Oral sex.

Sex is sex.

No matter which way you do it. And God's word is clear.

Flee from sexual immorality.

1 Corinthians 6:18

Embracing a life of purity isn't only about saying no to going all the way. Purity is also about:

How you think.

How you talk.

What you look at online.

What jokes you tell.

What jokes you choose to laugh at.

How you treat others.

What you do in your private world.

How can a young man keep his way pure?

By living according to your word.

Psalm 119:9

Chapter 7

MY FUTURE

Have you ever thought about how ridiculous the notion of palm reading is? To actually believe that someone can look at your hand, or any part of your body, and predict your future is absurd. Only God knows what the future holds, and He has designed a future uniquely for you. God wants nothing more than for you to fully experience **the life He has planned for you.** But to live your life to the fullest, you must first give Him all of you—your heart, dreams, priorities, desires, and, yes, even your palm.

Your future starts in  one second.

If you could write the perfect script for your future, what would it be?

Virgin until marriage, have kids with God-loving wife, good job to support, raise kids with church and no cussing, NO ALCHOHOL TILL 21, never drugs, Christian for life.

What steps are you taking now to make the dreams for your future become a reality?

Have you talked to God about your future?

Have you asked God what His desires are for your future? He has created you and has customized a future solely for you.

Write a prayer and ask God to show you His plans for your life.

Then pray daily that God will lead you to stay on track with His plan.

_____

_____

_____

_____

_____

_____

_____

_____

_____

If you died today, where would you spend eternity?

What do you think it takes to get into

Getting into Heaven isn't about being a good person. Because, by God's standards, none of us is good.

 "There is no one righteous, not even one."

Romans 3:10

The Bible explains that all of us are sinners, and because of that, we are separated from God.

 For all have sinned and fall short of the glory of God.

Romans 3:23

Because of our sin, we deserve death. Not just a physical death, but also a spiritual one. Meaning that when life is over for us on earth, we deserve to be separated forever from God.

 For the wages of sin is death.

Romans 6:23

Jesus died for you because this is the only way for you to have a relationship with God. Jesus died **in your place.**

But God demonstrates his own love for us in this: While we were still sinners, Christ died for us.

Romans 5:8

While on earth, Jesus made it clear that believing in Him is the only way to God—the only way to Heaven.

Jesus said, "I am the Road, also the Truth, also the Life. No one gets to the Father apart from me."

John 14:6 *(The Message)*

The Bible clearly spells it out for us:

1. Confess that you believe in Him and that you are lost without Him.

2. Believe in your heart that He is who He claimed to be: the Son of God.

If you confess with your mouth, "Jesus is Lord," and believe in your heart that God raised him from the dead, you will be saved. For it is with your heart that you believe and are justified, and it is with your mouth that you confess and are saved.

Romans 10:9–10

His promise is simple.

His promise is life-changing.

His promise is clear.

Everyone who calls on the name of the
Lord will be saved.

Romans 10:13

Can you remember a time when you have prayed and asked Jesus to take over your life? If not, pray this prayer:

Dear God,

I believe in you. I believe you created me and have a plan for my life. I believe your Son Jesus died for me on the cross and came back to life. I give you my life right now. Forgive me of my past mistakes and take over my life.

If you prayed this prayer and really mean it, then you have just crossed over from death to life. You have just made the most important decision of your life. Jesus is now living in you!

Giving your life to Jesus isn't the end.
It is only the beginning.

The journey begins now.